CHRIS TOMLIN
NEVER LOSE SIGHT

ISBN 978-1-4950-8058-6

HAL•LEONARD®

7777 W. BLUEMOUND RD. P.O. BOX 13819 MILWAUKEE, WI 53213

GOOD GOOD FATHER

Words and Music by PAT BARRETT
and ANTHONY BROWN

JESUS

Words and Music by CHRIS TOMLIN
and ED CASH

With praise

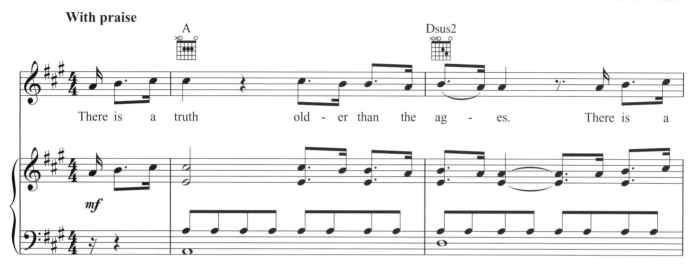

There is a truth old-er than the ag - es. There is a

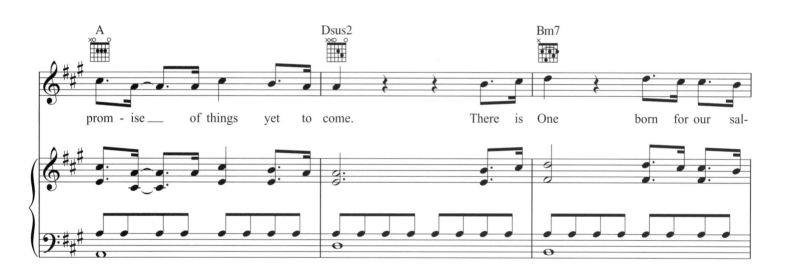

prom - ise __ of things yet to come. There is One born for our sal-

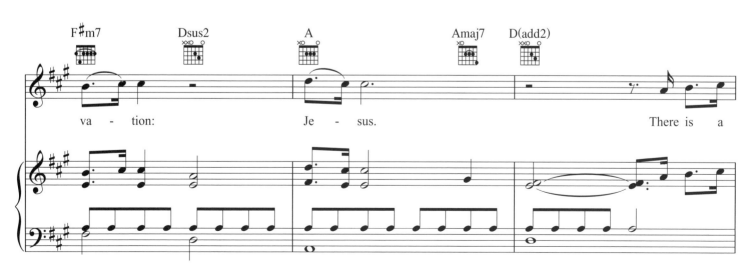

va - tion: Je - sus. There is a

IMPOSSIBLE THINGS

Words and Music by BRENTON BROWN,
CHRIS McCLARNEY, CHRIS TOMLIN
and ED CASH

HOME

Words and Music by CHRIS TOMLIN,
ED CASH and SCOTT CASH

GOD OF CALVARY

Words and Music by MATT REDMAN,
JONAS MYRIN, CHRIS TOMLIN
and MATT MAHER

Lyrics:

On the hill of Cal-va-ry, the light of all the world, with the world on __ His shoul-ders. __

The weight of all our shame on Him who knew no sin; a ho-ly __ sur-ren-der. __

On the hill of Cal-va-ry, in-to the Fa-ther's hands, a ho-ly __ sur-ren-der. __

* *Recorded a half step lower.*

HE LIVES

Words and Music by CHRIS TOMLIN,
BEN CANTELON, NICK HERBERT
and REUBEN MORGAN

Moderately slow

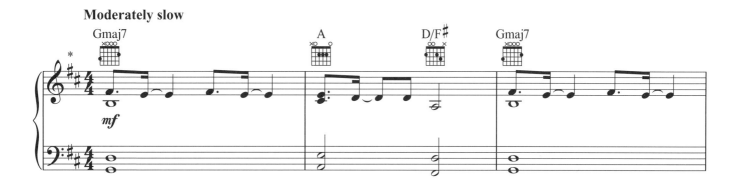

From heav - en ___ to earth our Sav - ior came. For
glo - ry ___ to Him up - on the throne, for -

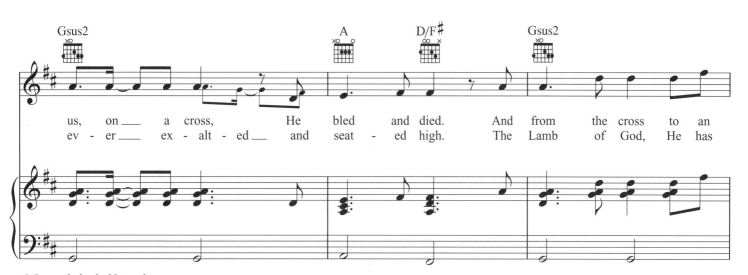

us, on ___ a cross, He bled and died. And from the cross to an
ev - er ___ ex - alt - ed ___ and seat - ed high. The Lamb of God, He has

* Recorded a half step lower.

GLORY BE

Words and Music by CHRIS TOMLIN,
JONAS MYRIN, ED CASH
and JASON INGRAM

COME THOU FOUNT
(I Will Sing)

Traditional Hymn
Lyrics by CHRIS TOMLIN

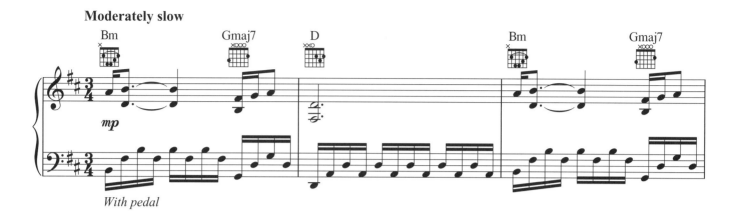

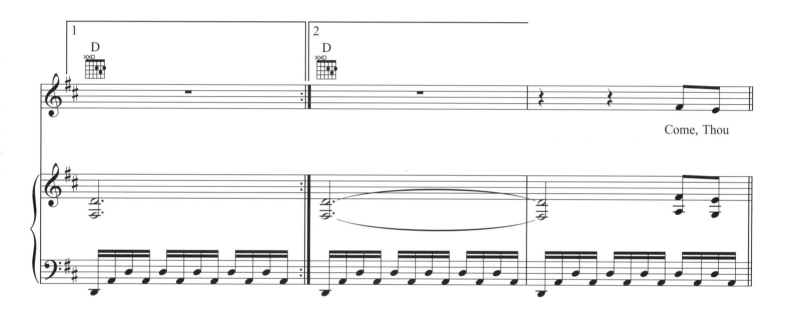

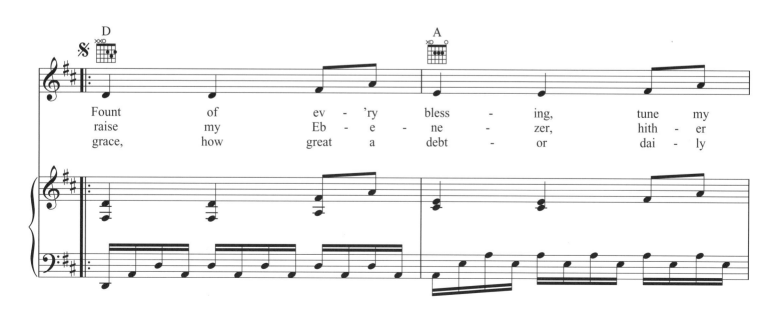

YES AND AMEN

Words and Music by CHRIS McCLARNEY,
NATE MOORE and ANTHONY BROWN

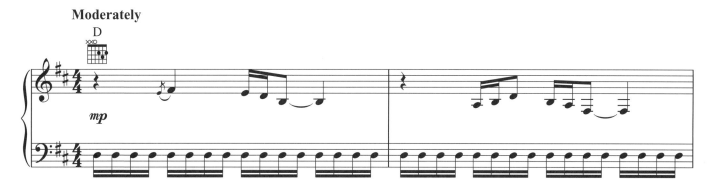

Fa - ther of kind - ness, You have poured out grace. _ You

brought me out _ of dark - ness, You have filled me _ with peace. _

To Coda

ALL YOURS

Words and Music by CHRIS TOMLIN,
REUBEN MORGAN, JESS CATES
and JASON INGRAM

You set the boun-d'ries for the o - ceans,
You com - mand the wind and _

God, You au - thored our be - gin - ning,
You have num - bered all our _

_ waves.
_ days.

Stand-ing o - ver ev-'ry sea - son, God, You reign, _

Your love for us is ev - er - last-ing be - yond the grave, _

You reign. _

You reign. _

And it's all Yours, the day and the night, _ the earth and the sky. _

FIRST LOVE

Words and Music by CHRIS TOMLIN,
MARTIN SMITH, REUBEN MORGAN
and KATHRYN SCOTT

THE GOD I KNOW

Words and Music by CHRIS TOMLIN,
ROSS COPPERMAN and JASON INGRAM

Recorded a half step lower.

GOD AND GOD ALONE

Words and Music by CHRIS TOMLIN,
JONAS MYRIN and JASON INGRAM

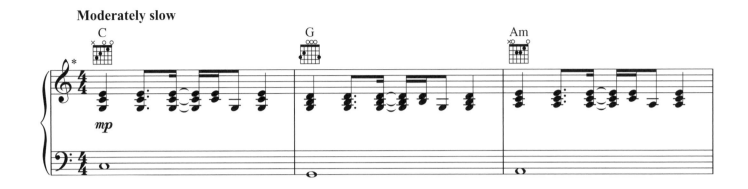

One church, one faith, one an-them raised. God and God a-
else can wash our sin a - way? God and God a -

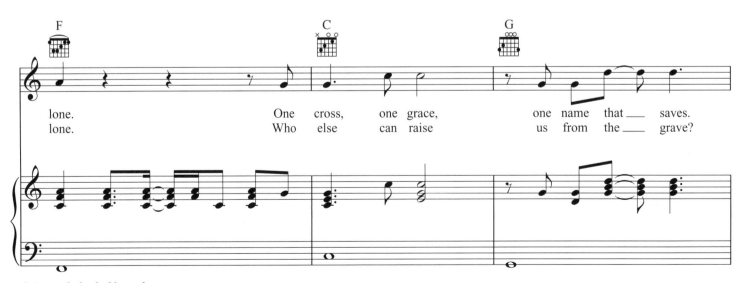

lone. One cross, one grace, one name that ___ saves.
lone. Who else can raise us from the ___ grave?

Recorded a half step lower.

KYRIE ELEISON

Words and Music by CHRIS TOMLIN,
MATT REDMAN, MATT MAHER
and JASON INGRAM